BRIEF

By the same author:

Side Effects (Peterloo Poets, 1978)

Standing To (Peterloo Poets, 1982)

Voices Off (Peterloo Poets, 1984)

Selected Poems (Peterloo Poets, 1986, hardcover & King Penguin, 1986, paperback)

A Watching Brief

U. A. FANTHORPE

PETERLOO POETS

First published in 1987
by Peterloo Poets
2 Kelly Gardens, Calstock, Cornwall PL18 9SA

ISBN 0 905291 87 5

Printed in Great Britain by
Latimer Trend & Company Ltd, Plymouth

ACKNOWLEDGEMENTS are due to the editors of *Critical Quarterly*, *Cumberland Poetry Review* (U.S.A), *Firebird*, *Outposts*, *The Pen*, *Poetry Book Society Supplement 1985/86* (ed. Carol Rumens), *Poetry Book Society Supplement 1986/87* (ed. Jonathan Barker), *Poetry Book Society Supplement 1987/88* (ed. Gillian Clarke) *Poetry Matters*, *Poetry Review*, *Proof*, *Prospice*, *Quaker Women's Group Newsletter*, *Spectator* and *Writing Women*, in whose pages some of these poems first appeared.

'Bakerloo' was commissioned by BBC English by Radio. 'The Doctor' was commissioned by The Tate Gallery and published in *With a Poet's Eye*. 'Dear Mr Lee' was commissioned by the Cheltenham Festival of Literature for a programme celebrating the life and work of Laurie Lee.

Ursula Fanthorpe would like to thank The Society of Authors for a £1,000 Travelling Scholarship for 1983, and The Arts Council, North West Arts and S.Martin's College, Lancaster, for a Writer's Fellowship, 1983–85. She writes:

> "It is hard to find words strong enough to convey thanks for so much friendship, hospitality, generosity and faith as came my way from staff and students at S.Martin's College and from writers and others in Lancaster and the north west."

for Rosemarie Bailey

Contents

OBSERVATIONS

WITNESSES

REMAINS

PERSPECTIVES

The Doctor

Sir Luke Fildes: *The Doctor*, Tate Gallery

'That Jackson, he's another one.
If he goes on opening windows we'll all
Die of pneumonia.'
The native obsessions:
Health and the weather. Attendants have
The dogged, grainy look of subjects. Someone,
Surely, is going to paint them?

'You don't have a bad heart yet, do you?'

'Not that I know of.'
'They can examine you.'

'But they don't really know.'
The painters knew.
Gainsborough eyed his lovely, delicate daughters
And rich fat brewers: Turner his hectic skies.
They brooded on death by drowning (Ophelia, in real water);
Cloud without end; storm; storm coming on;
Bright exophthalmic eyes, consumptive colours,
And gorgeous goitred throats; the deluge,
The end of the world, and Adam's
Appalling worm-wrapped birth.
Such patient watchers
Have eyes for those who watch. The child
Frets in its fever, the parents
Grieve in the background gloom. But the doctor,
Who has done all he can, and knows nothing
Will help or heal, sits raptly, raptly,
As if such absorbed attention were in itself
A virtue. As it is.

Downstairs at the Orangerie

I mount guard all day,
Feet apart in my correct shoes, arms crossed,
My mouth tucked into the policeman's slot,
Watching through powerful spectacles, listening
Through short-cut hair. For here,
Between the Maître and the Lion of France,
Rules are appropriate. Upstairs is different. With
Their disgusting nudes, their crazy Picassos, it is hard
To expect decorum. I have seen
Kissing upstairs, and worse. But here,
In my underwater world, I insist on etiquette.
Water-lilies are modest and delicate plants;
They cannot turn their heads and look away.
I protect their perpetual innocence. The Japanese
Can be relied on; there is some affinity
Between them and my children. But the Germans!
The Dutch! the faithless English! the dam-Yankees!
They move incessantly, they point, they speak aloud,
They touch. Criminal language, criminal behaviour.
I bark at them incomprehensibly: *N'touch'! C'est interdit!*
They flinch, but will not go. My waterlily world
Lives only in their absence. Then the still
And permanent things are eloquent
In their own way. I'm deaf to it,
But that is not important. I have my place.
I pace my precious, my mysterious world,
Master the frivolous mob, and bow my head
To Clemenceau and Monet as I pass
Their bearded busts. I keep the peace
Of this, their world and mine. I have
No oriflamme, no florid pose, no torch,
But I serve France.

La Débâcle. Temps Gris

Seine. Facing south. Mid-day.
No sun. Cloud heavy over Lavacourt,
No boat, no body. Water, ice, snow,
Houses, trees, hills, cloud, sky.

This picture means nothing
More than it shows. The tree standing alone
Is not me, though I understand
Why you might think so. Wrongly.

Not a thing here means
Anything but that it is here,
Now. I am the witness, bound to set down
What I see. This is what I see,

Watch. Begin with the water.
It is undisturbed. In it flower stilly
The crooked refractions of poplars.
The poplars grow up from underwater,

The poplars grow up from above water.
Ice and snow come between tree and reflection.
In this weather reflection does not grow into tree.
Ice bars it. Begin again with the water.

There is one ice-free patch. Here
The reflections are. Beyond, brash ice
That tomorrow will be free water.
I painted the water first, lying under.

Ice slabs jolt to edged poses:
Planks, tents, scrubbing brushes, gables,
Lobsters, slices of cake. Light on ice
Shines green, blue, yellow, red,

Rashers of colour run along
The slab-slides. Water and film and ice
Mirror the hummocky pink-grey cloud.
This is the moment. I have trapped it.

Moving did happen. Poplars
Were felled by snow; these can be seen.
An ice-clamped-solid reach can be deduced
From the gashed floes. People

Live in the houses, perhaps. I will not say.
I record what I see: the silent
Unclenching of the still-clenched river.
The Break-up of the Ice. The weather, grey.

Three Women Wordsworths

1. DEER IN GOWBARROW PARK

(for David Webb)

Not a gallant old warhorse of a poem,
Scarred from the student wars, but an indomitable
Little hackney, docile with twelve-year-olds,
Who may not understand *inner eyes* and
Tranquil recollecting, but know a *King Alfred*
When they see one, and can imagine lots.

Years later William knocked it together;
Mary gave her two lines. But it was Dorothy
Did the fieldwork, across the daffodilled years,
On a threatening misty morning, April,
1802. A boat is floating in the middle
Of the bay. Cows cause a diversion.
They see that yellow flower that Mrs C.
Calls *pilewort*; wood-sorrell; daffodils, naturally.

Waves at different distances, and rain,
And a sour landlady (*it is her way*),
And excellent ham and potatoes. Warm rum
And water for two—seven shillings all told.
We enjoyed ourselves, she says, *and wished*
For Mary. You hand us that day,

Dorothy, sister, all the random details, the furze bush
Opposite Mr Clarkson's, dry clothes afterwards,
William reading Congreve by the fire, how it rained
When you went to bed, and *N.B. Deer*
In Gowbarrow Park like skeletons,
With, of course, daffodils, *about the breadth*
Of a country turnpike road.

From William and Mary the official version,
Framed, in focus, ready to be declaimed,
Public as tapestry, concluding with a Thought.

The National Trust can use a poem like this.
But your straggle of unplanned delights and scrambles,
Texture of wind and wetness, glancing
Touch of the day, like (N.B.) the Gowbarrow deer
Defy the taming mind, your presence just
An urgent breathless charge: *N.B., N.B.*

2. UNDERCURRENTS AT THE DOVE AND OLIVE BOUGH

Complaint of the Guide:
All those portraits of Him, she says, not one of Her,
'Exquisite sister' with the wild eyes, only
One prim silhouette, image of Jane Austen,
And painful studies of senility.

Record of the House:
Sitting-room where the women clerked for William;
Bedroom lined with *The Times* to keep out damp,
Where children, sister slept, but not the Poet; door
William had built, *being disturbed*
By matters of a domestic nature.

Testimony of the Rug:
My wool is Grasmere wool,
Spun, dyed and knitted for the Poet's knees.
Rhubarb, mulberry, blackberry, old man's beard,
Begonia, nettles, privet, parsley, broom
She picked and steeped, poor feckless Willy's wife.
I represent long and unvalued hours
Of trivial effort. *It took some little time*,
She said of me.

Sign of the Sheepfold:
Built nearly in the form of a heart
Unequally divided.

3. THE LAST

'I shall forever feel thankful for the Almighty's goodness for having spared me to be the solitary lingerer.'
(Mary Wordsworth, 7th February, 1855)

She was a stayer-on, a knitter-up
Of others' untidy lives. Adept
At self-effacement, she shared honeymoon,
Husband, house, claimed nothing
For herself but to be of use.

Brother died, children died, adored adorable Dora
Died; Dorothy, incontinent and senile baby,
Farted and belched, shrieked, sang and swore and spat;
The most wonderful Friend in the world
Blurred and faded away.

At length even He died. And five years later
She died, *that poor Miss Wordsworth.*

Still she lived on, since somebody had to,
To name the Work and nurse it into print,
As he had known she would, dear Idiot Man,
With his bad nights, his love-child, his headaches,
Who never noticed things till Dorothy wrote them

Into his journal; was put right by eight-year-olds;
Couldn't take it in, the leech-gatherer's message; missed
The crowning moment when they crossed the Alps;
Whom she thanked tenderly after eight hard years of marriage
For *the first letter of love that has been*

Exclusively my own.

NOTES

These three poems are perhaps a gloss on Colderidge's remark about Wordsworth: 'living wholly among *Devotees*—having every the minutest Thing, almost his very Eating and Drinking, done for him by his Sister, or Wife.' I wasn't thinking about this remark when I wrote these poems, but it struck me afterwards. The more immediate cause was a visit to Dove Cottage at Grasmere. (U.A.F.)

1. DEER IN GOWBARROW PARK

The woman here is Dorothy, whose Journal entry for 15th April, 1802, was used by William to write the poem *Daffodils* in 1804.

Mary gave her two lines: Mary's lines are:

> 'They flash upon that inward eye
> Which is the bliss of solitude'.

2. UNDERCURRENTS AT THE DOVE AND OLIVE BOUGH

The woman here is Fanny, née Graham, wife of William's younger son Willy. His was not a successful career.
Dove Cottage was, before the Wordsworths came to it, a small pub called the Dove and Olive Bough. William refers to this in *The Waggoner* (1806):

> 'There, where the Dove and Olive Bough
> Once hung, a Poet harbours now,
> A simple water-drinking Bard . . .'

It was not generally regarded as a suitable house for a family, as it was so small.

painful studies of senility (line 5): by S. Crosthwaite (1833) and J. Harden (1842). Dorothy's Alzheimer's Disease seems to have become serious in 1829, when she was 58.

door (line 9): This was inserted while the Wordsworths lived here. It meant that William could walk straight from the garden to the sitting room without encountering the household working in the kitchen.

Built nearly in the form of a heart/Unequally divided (lines 22–23): Dorothy's description in her Journal (11th October, 1800) of the sheepfold which she and William went to look at that day. (The next day he began writing *Michael*.)

3. THE LAST
This woman is Mary Wordsworth (née Hutchinson). The epigraph is from a letter she wrote on 7th February, 1855, after Dorothy's death. William had died in 1850, Dorothy on 25th January, 1855.

The most wonderful Friend in the world (line 9): Coleridge (died 1834).

the Work (line 14): the 'poem on his own life', which he never gave a name to. Mary sent it to Moxon to be published under the title of *The Prelude*.

At Cowan Bridge

(for Elsa Corbluth)

This place has elected to lie low.
Houses are called *Private Road*
And *Private Property.*

Everything is ostentatiously eating:
Free-ranging hens and geese, a fat horse,
A goat tethered to its larder.
Black-snouted lambs nuzzle and crop.
The local store sells local lemon curd.
Two miles away at the teashop they hope
To delight your palate, and restore
Those jaded tastebuds.

And dandelions do well. Their mop heads stare
Up at the sun. But the scrawny ash
Hugs back its green.

Discreet of you not to die here,
Maria, Elizabeth, elder daughters,
Who caught death here.
The river's a true witness. It sings
A bleak song: children were cold here,
And children were hungry. The lion-headed fell
Averts its gaze, but you can see where winter
Has rubbed it raw. Here children died,

But were buried elsewhere. Here discretion
Is expected of the dead. Outside the chapel
Jesus assures the lunging lorries, in a dying fall,
I am the resurrection and the life
At Easter, in late hot April.
It makes no difference. Not many birds are singing.

What resurrection for the chilled children,
Blighted and broken, bundled home to die,
Killed off between July and June,
Silent singers, aged ten, aged nine?

Flesh is finished with. Something persists
In a sister, unrelenting, stunted;
In a dead child's voice outside a midnight window
Crying *Let me in, let me in.*

Here daffodils came
And have lived to regret it. In dwarfish clumps
They glower along the verge.

'These things were here'

(for Gladys Mary Coles)

And still are, Father. It is only
Your forging eye that's missing, water-watcher,
Weed-watcher, weather-watcher, Father head-in-air,

In this your cloud-capped county. (*My dear Baillie,*
The clouds are more interesting than in any other
Place I have been.) But for us, trailing you,

Summer sky was an unregenerate dull white over all.
(*Proper August weather*, snarled the natives.) No time
To visit your burly Ribble. But that grand barn

We did finally pitch on. Ill at ease
On holy ground, we trespassed into the wrong one,
Claimed to identify your great *A*s in the beams,

Knew privately this wasn't what had fetched you,
Asked a farmworker, sloshing through mud, one of your
Simple people, for whom beauty of inscape

Was buried away. Yes, he said, he knew which barn
It was, opened gates, walked us gravely through
(*There's a few cattle in, but you won't mind that*)

And there they were, as you saw them, the massive baulks
In high dimness above the dozy bullocks, vaulting adze-edged alphas,
Signifers for you of Who begins and ends. Here, Father,

As in so many places, you endured exile. (*My dearest Mother,*
By daylight I feel the strangeness of the place.) Yet here
In this great strange barn, which was also *ours*,

You found a likeness for the harvest-home
Of Christ, his mother, and all his hallows;

And for those whom your church could not then contain,
Those much loved holy heretics, *my dear Baillie,*
Dead *so dear to me* Henry Purcell, *dearest Bridges,*
My dear Canon, my dearest Mother,

And for those *simple people* who have hands to build
And eyes to see, who open gates, there seems here now to be
All the room in the world.

'July 19, 1872. Stepped into a barn of ours, a great shadowy barn, where the hay had been stacked on either side, and looking at the great rudely worked timberframes—principals(?) and tie-beams, which make them look like big bold *A*s with the cross-bar high up—I thought how sadly beauty of inscape was unknown and buried away from simple people and yet how near at hand it was if they had eyes to see it and it could be called out everywhere again . . .'

G. M. Hopkins's *Journal*

Dear Mr Lee

Dear Mr Lee (Mr Smart says
it's rude to call you Laurie, but that's
how I think of you, having lived with you
really all year), Dear Mr Lee
(Laurie) I just want you to know
I used to hate English, and Mr Smart
is roughly my least favourite person,
and as for Shakespeare (we're doing him too)
I think he's a national disaster, with all those jokes
that Mr Smart has to explain why they're jokes,
and even then no one thinks they're funny,
And T. Hughes and P. Larkin and that lot
in our anthology, not exactly a laugh a minute,
pretty gloomy really, so that's why
I wanted to say Dear Laurie (sorry) your book's
the one that made up for the others, if you
could see my copy you'd know it's lived
with me, stained with Coke and Kitkat
and when I had a cold, and I often
take you to bed with me to cheer me up
so Dear Laurie, I want to say sorry,
I didn't want to write a character-sketch
of your mother under headings, it seemed
wrong somehow when you'd made her so lovely,
and I didn't much like those questions
about *social welfare in the rural community*
and *the seasons as perceived by an adolescent*,
I didn't think you'd want your book
read that way, but bits of it I know by heart,
and I wish I had your uncles and your half-sisters
and lived in Slad, though Mr Smart says your view
of the class struggle is naïve, and the examiners
won't be impressed by me knowing so much by heart,
they'll be looking for terse and cogent answers
to their questions, but I'm not much good at terse and cogent,

I'd just like to be like you, not mind about being poor,
see everything bright and strange, the way you do,
and I've got the next one out of the Public Library,
about Spain, and I asked Mum about learning
to play the fiddle, but Mr Smart says Spain isn't
like that any more, it's all Timeshare villas
and Torremolinos, and how old were you
when you became a poet? (Mr Smart says for anyone
with my punctuation to consider poetry as a career
is enough to make the angels weep).

PS Dear Laurie, please don't feel guilty for
me failing the exam, it wasn't your fault,
it was mine, and Shakespeare's,
and maybe Mr Smart's, I still love *Cider*,
it hasn't made any difference.

'Very quiet here'

Picture postcard of Aldeburgh sent by Thomas Hardy to his sister, Kate Hardy, on 11th May, 1912

(for Bill Greenslade)

In Wessex no doubt the old habits resume:
Fair maidens seduced in their innocent bloom,
May-month for suicide, and other crimes
(Two Dorchester murders discussed in *The Times*),
Mutilation of corpses, infanticide, rape,
And so many reasons for purchasing crêpe.
All stirring at home. But here vacancy reigns;
I have nothing to watch but my varicose veins.

Very quiet here.
Not an apprentice has perished this year.

I envy Crabbe the matter that he saw:
Those wasting ills peculiar to the poor,
Decline and dissolution, debts and duns,
The dreary marshes and the pallid suns—
So much for him to write about. And I
In Wessex homely ironies can spy.

None of that here.
Even dear Emma a trifle less queer.

Deck-chaired and straw-hatted I sit at my ease,
With each blighted prospect determined to please.
Inside my old skin I feel hope running on—
Perhaps a changed life when poor Emma is gone?
Strange foreknowings fret me: guns, music and war,
A corpse with no heart, a young Briton ashore
Walks here where I sit with the atheist Clodd,
Discussing the quirks of that local cult, God.

I ponder how
Time Past and Time to Come pester me now.

CALLINGS

At Averham

Here my four-year-old father opened a gate,
And cows meandered through into the wrong field.

I forget who told me this. Not, I think,
My sometimes reticent father. Not much I know

About the childhood of that only child. Just
How to pronounce the name, sweetly deceitful

In its blunt spelling, and how Trent
Was his first river. Still here, but the church

Closed now, graveyard long-grassed,
No one to ask in the village. Somewhere here,

I suppose, I have a great-grandfather buried,
Of whom nothing is known but that, dying, he called

My father's mother from Kent to be forgiven.
She came, and was. And came again

To her sister, my great-aunt, for
Her dying pardon too. So my chatty mother,

But couldn't tell what needed so much forgiving,
Or such conclusive journeys to this place.

Your father, pampered only brother
Of many elder sisters, four miles away,

Grew up to scull on this river. My father,
Transplanted, grew up near poets and palaces,

Changed Trent for Thames. Water was in his blood;
In a dry part of Kent his telephone exchange

Was a river's name; he went down to die
Where Arun and Adur run out to the sea.

Your father, going north, abandoned skiffs for cars,
And lived and died on the wind-blasted North Sea shore.

They might have met, two cherished children,
Among nurses and buttercups, by the still silver Trent,

But didn't. That other implacable river, war,
Trawled them both in its heady race

Into quick-march regiments. I don't suppose they met
On any front. They found our mothers instead.

So here I stand, where ignorance begins,
In the abandoned churchyard by the river,

And think of my father, his mother, her father,
Your father, and you. Two fathers who never met,

Two daughters who did. One boy went north, one south,
Like the start of an old tale. Confusions

Of memory rise: rowing, and rumours of war,
And war, and peace; the secret in-fighting

That is called marriage. And children, children,
Born by other rivers, streaming in other directions.

You like the sound of my father. He would
Have loved you plainly, for loving me.

Reconciliation is for the quick, quickly. There isn't enough
Love yet in the world for any to run to waste.

Sounds and Silences

(for David)

Sound heard only in childhood:
Interminable mumbling like rock-doves
Over early-morning tea, after last night's differences,
Of parents in their bedroom, creating today.

Conversations we might have had,
But didn't; the smothered grievances:
She loves you better than me; You
With your nose in a book. The uncleared air.

Scraps of learning stage-managed
To impress outsiders: cycling through tolerant suburbs
Shrieking bad extrovert French, playing
At being other; postcards in cuneiform.

Unplanned confidings of drunkenness
Which, as sobriety settles, we conspire
To forget. The mazy toastings
Of deadest philosophers, most indifferent stars.

Stalking neglected churches on unpretending
Bedfordshire uplands, your moped illegal,
Exhaustless. Conversation was basic shouts,
Small talk about roodlofts.

Drowned utterance of your just-got-home self,
Shrugging off the commuter, communing with terrapins
And watersnails. Silence eddied round you.
I watched; tried not to see.

Distant arpeggios of our mother playing
Rustle of Spring downstairs, at night, after dinner.
We listened, scared. Did she mean
To charm our childhood, or retrace her own?

Was she playing perhaps because she was happy?
Why did the innocent tinkle alarm us?
Where were we going?

A Wartime Education

Lessons with Mam'zelle were difficult.
Le général would crop up in the middle of
The most innocent Daudet. Tears for *la France*,
La belle France embarrassed our recitation
Of nouns with tricky plurals: hibou, chou, *hélas*, bijou.

A father in uniform conferred status. Mine,
Camping it up with the Home Guard in Kent
On summer nights, too human for heroics.

Bananas and oranges, fruit of triumphant
Decimated convoys, were amazements
Of colour and light, too beautiful to eat.
(In any case, eating three bananas
Straight off, one after the other,
Was certain death. We all knew that.)

Struggling through adolescence, trying
To accommodate Macbeth, parents, God,
Teachers of mathematics, it was hard
To sustain plain hatred for *the Hun*,

Known only as nightly whines, searchlights, thuds, bomb-sites.
Might he not, like Aeneas, have reasons
(Insufficient, but understandable) for what he did?
I found it hard to remember which side

I was on, argued endlessly at home,
Once, rashly, in a bus, and had to be defended
By mother from a war-widow. *Careless talk*
Costs lives warned the posters. I had no secrets

To offer, but acquired a habit of
Permanent secrecy, never admitted
How I hated the wolf-whistling lorry-loaded
Soldiers, passing me *en route* to D-day.

Washing-up

(for Hilda Cotterill)

Our mother, hater of parties and occasions,
Made much of the washing-up after. It became an exorcising,
A celebration. Outsiders gone, the kitchen choked
With leftovers, disordered courses, mucky fiddly forks,
The alarming best glasses. She worked a system,
A competition. First we stacked the mess
In regular order: glasses, cutlery, plates
(Each in their kind); saucepans and base things last.

Then we began. She washed, I wiped; to the first to finish,
The prize of *putting-away*. A wiper-up
Should finish first. I never did, for mother
Slaved in a bacchic frenzy, scattering Vim
And purity, splashing new libations
Of suds and scalding water, piling with exquisite fingers
(Unringed for the occasion) the china in ranks,
Knives all together. I was made slow by her passion.

And as we worked she sang. My doughty mother—
Who lived through wars and took life seriously,
Never read fiction, seldom laughed at jokes—
My sorcerer-mother sang grand opera,
Parodied makeshift words and proper music.
Softly awoke her heart, without too much bathos,
But *Samso-o-o-n* got her going, and she never
Took *Travatore* seriously: *Ah, I have sighed to rest me*
Deep in the quiet grave she'd serenade
The carving-knife, from that a short step
To saucepans and the Jewel Song: *Marguerita, this is not I.*
High-born maiden I must be, high-born maiden . . .
Her mezzo skidding along coloratura country,
My laughter rattling the stacks. The men
Came down to hear. And as she nipped
Between cupboards (having won), she added the footwork
Of humbler songs: *Home James, and don't spare*
The horses. This night has been ruin for me. Home James,
And don't spare the horses. I'm ruined as ruined can be

With a pert little mime. She liked these ruined maids,
Or about to be. *No! No! A thousand times no!*
You cannot buy my caress. No! No! A thousand times no!
I'd rather die than say yes. But her feet denied it.

Lastly, when all was done, her party-piece
True to the self she seldom let us see:
I feel so silly when the moon comes out . . .
Then, everything purged and placed, we'd go to bed.

O I remember my magical mother dancing
And singing after the party, under the airer
With the used tea towels hanging up to dry.

Eating Out

Adventures into rehearsed but unknown living,
Table napkin tucked conscientiously under chin.

Choice of cutlery supervised, menu explained.
So much good behaviour was indigestible;

Mother took me outside to recover. Later,
Father introduced London cuisine:

How to handle *moules marinière*, not
To eat all the *petits fours*, or pocket them for later.

When the proper time came, he initiated me
Into the ritual consumption of lobster.

My last outing with him: teacakes in
A Petworth teashop. He leaned heavy on my arm,

But did the ordering. Mother died older, later;
I never accustomed myself to this autocrat's

Humble *I'll have whatever you're having, dear.*

7301

Learning to read you, twenty years ago,
Over the pub lunch cheese-and-onion rolls.

Learning you eat raw onions; learning your taste
For obscurity, how you encode teachers and classrooms

As *the hands, the shop-floor*; learning to hide
The sudden shining naked looks of love. And thinking

The rest of our lives, the rest of our lives
Doing perfectly ordinary things together—riding

In buses, walking in Sainsbury's, sitting
In pubs eating cheese-and-onion rolls,

All those tomorrows. Now twenty years after,
We've had seventy-three hundred of them, and

(If your arithmetic's right, and our luck) we may
Fairly reckon on seventy-three hundred more.

I hold them crammed in my arms, colossal crops
Of shining tomorrows that may never happen,

But may they! Still learning to read you,
To hear what it is you're saying, to master the code.

Old Man, Old Man

He lives in a world of small recalcitrant
Things in bottles, with tacky labels. He was always
A man who did-it-himself.

Now his hands shamble among clues
He left for himself when he saw better,
And small things distress: *I've lost the hammer.*

Lifelong adjuster of environments,
Lord once of shed, garage and garden,
Each with its proper complement of tackle,

World authority on twelve different
Sorts of glue, connoisseur of nuts
And bolts, not good with daughters

But a dab hand with the Black and Decker,
Self-demoted in your nineties to washing-up
After supper, and missing crusted streaks

Of food on plates; have you forgotten
The jokes you no longer tell, as you forget
If you've smoked your timetabled cigarette?

Now television has no power to arouse
Your surliness; your wife could replace on the walls
Those pictures of disinherited children,

And you wouldn't know. Now you ramble
In your talk around London districts, fretting
At how to find your way from Holborn to Soho,

And where is Drury Lane? Old man, old man,
So obdurate in your contracted world,
Living in almost-dark, *I can see you,*

You said to me, *but only as a cloud.*
When I left, you tried not to cry. I love
Your helplessness, you who hate being helpless.

Let me find your hammer. Let me
Walk with you to Drury Lane. I am only a cloud.

Queuing outside the Jeu de Paume in light rain

If you were here
I'd ask the smiling African
In my slow-motion French what makes his birds
Rattle their paper wings, and fly, and fall
Beside his hand. *Gilly-gilly-gilly*, he woos us all,
Very good, very nice. For you he'd laugh,
And tell.

If you were here
Something profound about his airy art,
The art we queue for under our umbrellas,
Would bounce between us, jokily. You'd note
The grace of our neighbours' passing-the-time conversation
(*Mind you, Muriel says it's always raining in Paris,
And she lives here*).

I have grown expert on your absences. I know
How things would differ, how the resolute
Mock-bird would tangle frailly with my feet,
And how you'd buy it, just because it did,
And you were there.

Difficilior lectio

'thaes ofereode, thisses swa maeg' (*Deor*)

Absence is incontinent. It leaves
Shaming wet patches in obvious places.
Some people cry easily. I am one.

Not you.

Study of Old English, under legendary masters,
I took to be an advantage. So many years later
That all I can safely remember is a *hwaet* or so,
I can't eliminate the aura of authority,

Claim to understand the ancestral mind,
How it was always defeat that moved them; how, if the hero
Killed a dragon or two, there was always
A final one coming; how to be on the winning side

Was dull, and also misleading. You, who read translations,
Speak humbly of their world. I catch you
House-training the dragon, my absence, with small
Jokes, diet of liver and onions, digging
A vegetable patch, reading my old books.

Why, I ask, *why the Anglo-Saxons*?

Because, you said, *they understand exile*.

Looking for Jorvik

Veterans swap yarns about how long they queued
In the rain to see Tutankhamun.

Sweet summer York is nothing. They dip alertly
Into the dark, the time capsule. (*No dogs,*

Smoking, ice-cream, cameras.) History
Breathes them in, past *Pack up your troubles,*

Puffing billies, factory acts, perukes, Marston Moor,
(*Have you got a sweety, Geoffrey love?*)

Mendicant friars, the Black Death, through the one
Date everybody knows, to the ancestral

Mutter and reek. This is then, now. We are
Where it was, it is. (*There's a man as big*

As a troll at the door.) Here the foundations are,
Pit, mud, stumps, the endless tons of bones,

Tiny dark plum stones of Viking York.
(And he said *I dabbled my blade in*

Bloodaxe's boy.) At this level the appalling
Icelander Egil who must not be killed at night

(*Night-killings are murder*) saved his neck by his
Head-Ransom song next day. And got off.

As we do, in the souvenir shop. *That wouldn't*
Interest me. But for someone like Barbara,

Who's a real intellectual . . . She was an English teacher,
You know. T shirts, baseball caps, keyrings, tapestry kits,

Activity packs proclaim *Eric Bloodaxe Rules OK*. And I
Have unearthed my own past under Jorvik's shaft,

Changing trains twenty years ago on York station at midnight
Among kit-bagged soldiers, on my way to you, thinking suddenly:

I am on my way to life.

Note:
In 948, Egil had been shipwrecked off the Yorkshire coast, and knew he could expect no mercy from Eric Bloodaxe, who ruled York, because he had killed Eric's son. The rules of that society prevented Eric from having Egil put to death at once, because he had arrived after dark, so Egil was given the chance of composing overnight his Head-Ransom song (20 stanzas in praise of Eric). This, because it was so brilliant, forced Eric to grant Egil his life.

Dear True Love

Leaping and dancing
Means to-ing and fro-ing;
Drummers and pipers—
Loud banging and blowing;
Even a pear-tree
Needs room to grow in.

Goose eggs and gold top
When I'm trying to slim?
And seven swans swimming?
Where could they swim?

Mine is a small house,
Your gifts are grand;
One ring at a time
Is enough for this hand.

Hens, colly birds, doves—
A gastronome's treat.
But love, I did tell you,
I've given up meat.

Your fairy-tale presents
Are wasted on me.
Just send me your love
And set all the birds free.

Confessio Amantis

Because I know who you are
Up to a point:—you are
Martha, who feels ashamed
Of merely doing; Atlas,
Who uncomplaining keeps off the fearful
Skies from the cringing earth
With the palms of his hands
For ever, without mentioning it, so that he appears
To be a mountain rather than a man;
Martha, the handyman of the Lord,
Up to a point;
                    therefore to you
I will confess my own name. I am Dog
Who loves mankind but must also
Bark at the gate; I am Dragon,
Mythical, absurd, with wings; I am also
Watchman, who waketh, generally without a clue
Of what he waketh for; and I am Spy,
Watchman's other self, the double agent,
The fifth column who has lost touch
With the other four. And I am the fifth column
(Which is unnecessary) who is the Fool,
Full of wise saws and modern instances,
Babbling away irrelevant, incoherent,
In the world's apocalyptic thunderstorm

Up to a point.

Homing In

Somewhere overseas England are struggling
On a sticky wicket; somewhere in Europe
An elder statesman is dying *adagio*; and here,
Nowhere precisely, I slip to pips and bens
Through the occupied air.

Somewhere along this road an invisible ditch
Signals tribe's end, an important mutation of [ʌ];
Somewhere among these implacable place-names
People are living coherent lives. For me the unfocussed
Landscape of exile.

Somewhere along this watershed weather
Will assert itself, swap wet for dry,
Scribble or flare on windscreens, send freak gusts
Sneaking round juggernauts, ravel traffic with
A long foggy finger.

Home starts at Birmingham. Places
Where I have walked are my auguries:
The stagey Malverns, watery sharp Bredon,
May Hill's arboreal quiff. These as I pass
Will bring me luck if they look my way.

I should be rehearsing contingencies,
Making resolutions, allowing for change
In the tricky minor modes of love. But,
Absorbed by nearly-home names,
Dear absurd Saul, Framilode, Frampton-on-Severn,

I drop, unprepared, into one particular
Parish, one street, one house, one you,
Exact, ignorant and faithful as swallows commuting
From Sahara to garage shelf.

Teacher's Christmas

It's not so much the ones whose cards don't come,
Friends of one's parents, old distinguished colleagues
Who taught the colonies and, retiring home,
Did a spot of dignified coaching. Their sudden silence
Is a well-bred withdrawing, not unexpected.

But those who move from address to more sheltered address,
Whose writing gutters gently year by year,
Whose *still hoping to see you again* after *love*
Is bluff; or those who write after Christmas
Because *cards are so expensive now*. Ah those, how those

Punctiliously chart their long decline.

The stages grow familiar, like disease.
First it's *my dauntless Mini, less staunch now,*
But I could come by bus, with sandwiches.
I shall enjoy the jaunt.

WEA classes go. Then television
Becomes remote, and radio's
Hard for the hard of hearing. Still they write,
They write at Christmas. Prithee, good death's-heads,
Bid me not remember mine end.

Season as well of cards from brilliant girls,
A little less incisive every year,
Reporting comings, goings: another Hannah,
Another Jamie; another husband going off; and
Writing my thesis is like digging a well with a pin.

You, the storm-troopers of a newer, better world.

Down with you, holly. Come down, ivy.

S. Martin's College, Lancaster

(for Robert Clayton)

Sword into felt-tip, Mars into Martin
The Oxfam saint. It's true about plough-shares:
Almost anything warlike, kept long enough,

Rusts into use. Armoury was where library is,
Since books are dangerous as bayonets,
And keep their point longer. Where officers

And gentlemen once toasted *The King the Duke*,
Bragged about whores and horses, the soft
Uncritical hum of the photocopier, plans

For peaceful teaching practice manoeuvres
In Morecambe. Inside the compound the urgent
Dilatory promenade of study, irregular presence

Of willow and flowering crab, where other ranks
Stamped their exact angles, angled their eyes
As the sergeant told them. Gone, all gone.

Now on the barrack square the chapel's shaft,
Collecting eyes like an after-dinner hostess,
Suggests a move elsewhere; in the keep now

TV's inhuman eye invigilates. Only the dumb
Dangling ghost of the suicidal batman
Still persists, and the guard-room dogs,

Nab de Cordova and Bob, unfailing garrison,
In their regimental graves, in the old tradition.
Two chiselled Lancashire roses. No flag; not a drum.

In Residence

(for Anita Mason)

Watcher by the wordhoard, waiting
Alone for the lightning, the long night
When patterns show plain as parsley
And pen knows its way along paper;

Sentry over old songs and nothing-special,
Exiled to not-explaining, expected to do well,
Sentenced to endless hospitality of the innocent,
Trying not to bite, to be human;

Envier of other lives, evenly earthed
In mothers-in-law, milkmen, catchment areas,
Of their open fires, elderly cats, allotments,
So solidly dictated by the district;

Alien uncamouflaged and only,
Constant odd number at the kindly tables,
Idle, inquisitive, untrustworthy;

The writer wriggles inside the residence.

Looking for Patterns at Half Moon Bay

The sea is making a delayed entry.
It says *Heysham, Heysham, Heysham,*
In a wet voice.

A large white dog gallumphs down the sand
Looking for someone to relate to. Its footprints
Are bigger than its feet, and fitted
With sandy footnotes.

Miss Woodward is keen on that sort of thing.
It must be good for the children.

Above the shore line mud-bonded striations
Majestically expose themselves, as if they were for sale.

Someone is talking about student contact time.
There is also timetable time, high tide time,
Opening time and time. High tide time
Ticks silently round us, a bomb in water.

The sea leaves different clues for different students:
A hypodermic, a milk crate, an industrial glove,
A comprehensive dusting of feathers, bones, shells,
And a pair of scissors in the lotus position.

The musician walks at the water's edge,
Talking to his recorder. He might be studying
The pulse and pitch of the sea.

The students are conscious of their situation.
One of them says: *Are you studying us?*

Bin-bags hold the things that can be handled.
A mattress has to be carried separately,
And memories, tenuous, enormous, are piled
Inside the brain. Bin-bags
May be left in the Art department.

Inside each brain there's a little clerk
Stacking, labelling, storing, making sense;
Doing overtime today.

Going Down

(for Kate Macher)

Who in the library dump books and stand as if waiting.
Ten minutes later still standing, still as if waiting.

Ending's an art. In symphonies, those slamming
Incontrovertible chords cue in the cheers.

Three years' Top Twenties will always conjure up
This place, these no-more selves. Initiation

Would make it easier: clowning in fancy dress,
Vigil, carnival, balloons going up and away.

Instead, a formal dinner: bare backs, bow ties,
I pray you be upstanding . . . comic speech by the Bursar.

A disco, too loud for truth, too bright for facing eyes.
Swapping addresses with friends they won't be writing to.

Tutors are no help. Hands clasped guiltily, knowing
How much failure lies in the sweat between palms.

A heatwave now is inexcusable. Buildings
Preen in the sun, and first years sprawl on lawns.

No, I haven't exactly got a job . . . to find myself . . .
We're neither of us sure . . . Cloud nine should be close,

But all that's heard is a quiet voice saying
I think I ought to go and get a bottle of wine,

And parents are waiting at home with questions:
Well, what is it you've got? What's a Two-One, then?

Off Sick

Regime of the house: the sun's morning
Tour, his unsuspected finger on a dim corner.

The house is not primed for my presence. I intrude
On it's private life. Forgive me, house,

My excuse is fever. You can disregard me.
If I were myself I should not be here.

My true world is dancing to its own
Metronome: mail, first clinic, coffee-break,

FEM's letters. Someone there is being me,
Not perfectly, I hope. I sweat to think

They imagine me malingering, may fancy
I enjoy this fretting leisure, place of estrangement.

Resignation Letter

I am cartographer of the dull incline
Which all who visit choose to leave and forget.

I am on nodding terms with explorers of
The Rolandic Fissure, the Optic Chiasm, the Island of Reil.

I can guide the helpless to the lavatory,
The patients' canteen, the bus back to the centre.

I can interpret the hieroglyphs of initiates.
In the R ½sphere the 9–10 Hz alpha rhythm

At 30–60 uv in amp. means nothing to me,
But I can decode it. My name is Pomp.

Circumstance is what I am paid to prevent.
It's all very well for you. Your sex life

Is probably all right is the sort of thing patients want
To shout at consultants. My job: to ensure that they don't.

I am keeper of keys and secrets. I am familiar
With high IQs and low grade mental defectives.

I am acquainted with the smells of grief,
Panic, obsession, incontinence, apathy.

I understand the meaning of expensive florists' bouquets
On patients' birthdays, and no visitors.

I know how to speak to ambulance men:
Flattery, gratitude, abject femininity. Never cap their jokes.

I have composed a full scale commination service
For those who interrupt receptionists' coffee breaks,

Or say *Easy for some.* It is not easy.
I know too much, remember too much. It is time to go.

OBSERVATIONS

Halley's Comet 1985–86

(in honour of Patrick Moore)

Written at the request of Cleone, Viscountess Parker, for her children, Tanya, Katharine and Marian, descendants of George Parker, 2nd Earl of Macclesfield, astronomer, who was responsible for Britain's adoption of the Gregorian calendar.

I am the long-haired athlete of the sky,
Always predictable, never quite precise.

Who lives to see me twice
Lives to be old.

Many kept vigil for me: Chinese astronomers
With their strong bare eyes; Harold
And his star-crossed Saxons, stitched
Into history deciphering disaster
From my tail; candid Giotto of the perfect circle
Showed me tacitly on fresco; and Kepler knew me,
Walking home at midnight from a party.

Men without telescopes or truthful clocks.

Then Halley named me and reckoned my route.

Heavenly eccentric, syncopating centuries,
I visit dearest Earth, so green and blue and small,
Looping my orbit round her hemispheres,
Springing past Sun to beyond-sight Neptune,
Slow and more slow, and lagging as I spin,
Then widdershins back, towards new techniques,
New signs of love. Earth shines more bright for me.

This time my lover sends me dancing-partners
Whom I shall shatter in my dusty unveiling.

For those I favour are the patient men
Who watch, who wait, show children where to find me.

Travelling Man

Wonderful where you can go nowadays
(He says). Where you can go,
What you can learn. It wer Portugal
This year for us (he says).

Now the wife, she gets a bit bored like
Wi' culture. But me,
I wanted to see Wellington's campaign
Int' flesh, you might say.

'Course, being a package tour, we only
Went where they took us.
But magic places, magic. Porto, now,
And Jerez. I liked Jerez.

Last year it wer Italy. Vesuvius
(All that lava, y'know) and Pompey,
And Rome. Wonderful, wonderful!
And Sorrento. What a name!

I couldn't lie about on beaches
(He says). I like to see t'sights.
But I feel guilty about th'owd uns.
They din't ave these chances.

Me grandparents, y'know. I feel guilty
They din't see this,
They din't gerrabout. Me grandmother,
When she cum from Blackpool to see us,

She allus said *I ave to be ome at night*
To get t'meat (cheap cuts, that were, y'know).
She wouldn't ave wanted. And me mother,
She just laughs at me feelin guilty.

She says *Your father ud never*
Sleep in a strange bed.

Sunderland Point and Ribchester

Sunderland Point, where sea, wind, sky
Dispute dominion, on a spur of land
So bitter that you'd think no one would take
The trouble to go there.
                                        Here SAMBO lies,
A faithful NEGRO, who (attending his Mafter
From the Weft Indies) DIED
On his Arrival at Sunderland.

It is, of course, unconsecrated ground.

Now children stagger here on pilgrimage,
Their offerings the sort of things you'd find
On a pet's grave: a cross of driftwood, lashed
With binder-twine; a Woolworth vase,
Chocked up with grit and pebbles, crammed
With dead wild flowers.
                                        Sam lies very low.
You can allow him any voice you like.
Despair, pneumonia, exile, love, are variously
Thought to have killed him. A good place
To bring the kids in summer at weekends.

Ribchester had a stone, now lost.
Camden preserved the proper idiom:
By this earth is covered she who was once
Aelia Matrona, who lived 28 years, 2 months,
And 8 days, and Marcus Julius Maximus,
Her son, who lived 6 years, 3 months,
And 20 days.
                              A place to bring the kids.

Children are the most authentic
Pilgrims, having farthest to go, and knowing
Least the way.
                              The Romans understood
The use and pathos of arithmetic.

And the Ribble bites its banks, and the sea gnaws at the shore.
So many patterns gone, the *faithful slave*, the *son*
Most dutiful to his father. The word
Strives to be faithful, but the elements
Are against it.
We are all exiles, Sam,
From the almost-forgotten country
Before the divorce, before the failed exam,
Before the accident, before the white man came.
Your situation's more extreme than most,
But we all of us, all of us seek
That country. And you, who so clearly were not
Your own man, lying in no man's land,
A journey's end for children, seem in your muteness
To be meaning something.
Alternative:
The massive Roman formulas: *the century*
Of Titius built 27 feet . . .
. . . According to the reply of the god.

First Flight

Plane moves. I don't like the feel of it.
In a car I'd suspect low tyre pressure.

A sudden swiftness, earth slithers
Off at an angle. The experienced solidly

This is rather a short hop for me

Read *Guardians*, discuss secretaries,
Business lunches. I crane for the last of dear

I'm doing it just to say I've done it

Familiar England, motorways, reservoir,
Building sites. Nimble tiny disc, a sun

Tell us when we get to water

Runs up the porthole and vanishes.
Under us the broad meringue kingdom

The next lot of water'll be the Med

Of cumulus, bearing the crinkled tangerine stain
That light spreads on an evening sea at home.

You don't need an overcoat, but
It's the sort of place where you need
A pullover. Know what I mean?

We have come too high for history.
Where we are now deals only with tomorrow,
Confounds the forecasters, dismisses clocks.

My last trip was Beijing. Know where that is?
Beijing. Peking, you'd say. Three weeks there, I was.
Peking is wrong. If you've been there
You call it Beijing, like me. Go on, say it.

Mackerel wigs dispense the justice of air.
At this height nothing lives. Too cold. Too near the sun.

Carthage: an historical guide

'Dux femina facti' (Aeneid 1, 264)
'A woman led the exploit' (tr. C. Day Lewis)

Respect the time! she cautions, *respect the time!*
In all my years as guide, I lose only one person.
Now you must synchronise your watches.

Wheat grows between oranges. Massive lemon trees
Bow under yellow heavyweights. Vines in March,
Pruned grasping gnarls.

Story of Dido and the bullhide.
She was intelligent! (meaning—almost French).
The Romans emerge without credit,

Irrational, short-memoried. *They hated this place!*
The ten-day holocaust, the sowing with salt,
The solemn imprecations,

And then they went and rebuilt it. *Next came the Vandals,*
And you can forget those people for history.
As for today, we should notice

Very wild driving what the Tunisians do.
They have the mirror to look at the hair,
Not at the car behind.

They are poor, we must understand. *You have money,*
You can live. If not, it is for you
Bread and olives.

The Phoenicians she approves. Child sacrifice, certainly,
But only in the best families, and
It was for the Commerce.

We are to read *Salammbô*, distinguished work
Of Flaubert, celebrated novelist
(Who was, of course, French).

Now at La Goulette we must notice flamingos,
Men trawling snails, the Turkish fort where Christians
Scorched until sold,

And finally, Dido's headland, where she flared
Into legend. Not, we are glad to learn,
For frail Aeneas' sake,

But prudently, as a true Frenchwoman would,
For the Commerce, so that her people might be briefly sure
Of olives, freedom, bread.

Terminal Feelings

Like coming late to a tough public school.
They all know the rules except me,
And watch my mistakes coldly, knowingly.

I am body-searched. Judiciously she avoids
My erogenous zones, takes my word

That the bulge in my pocket is four pens:
Even as a terrorist not taken seriously.

I will not ask my way to the Ladies
Of blackhaired silent women or smiling brown men.

A prefect takes pity on me in the Duty Free,
Where expert hands clutch Harrods carriers,

Cases of Glenfiddich, smoked salmon sandwiches.
I emerge with a film, a blush, an orange juice.

Authority intones a lesson of boarding tickets and gates.
The native language sounds kinder in French:
Priez vous présenter . . .

Everyone approachable proves incomprehensible.
Why does no one want my passport?

Surely the air-hostesses will be
Miss Temples of the air, gentle, wise,

Offering me toilet facilities and hot
Buttered toast, cut small? But no,

They are sweet-centred Tunisian dates,
Smilers only at men.

WITNESSES

Rag Trade

(for Diana Hendry)

Winter is exclusive. Such shape-defining whiteness
Can be worn only by the fine-boned, the unsoiled.

Spring is proverbially cruel. That special yellow
Kills all but the most invincible complexions.

And the variations on green that summer
Unendingly designs. Redheads alone can live with them.

But autumn, with her Blood-and-Bile range,
Her crêpy textures. We all gravitate to her house.

Of Mutability

(for Meg)

Granted the fragility of Maran chicks,
New goslings, a twelve-year-old willing dog,
An arthritic right hand; granted the staying power
Of dock, cow-parsley, slurry; of this world's weather,
The helm wind. There is also a knack
Of enduring. This house was built because of it.
And since vocation hauled you unceremoniously
Here, from all the usual sweet concerns of life,
To breathe among curlews, between limestone and sandstone,
I see that something is expected of you here.

Cats will kill swallows; the finite scenes
Of birth and death recur. But things done,
Meals cooked, fires lit, trees planted, words said,
Poems observed, have their own posterity,
Though dreams may deny it. In such cold harbours
What's done is meant, and being meant, it stays.

M.S.

There is a small dead tree in the aviary
For them to perch on. But the aviary's closed.
(*Too cold yet, I suppose*, she says, though we're drinking
Tea in the garden.) Two and a half pair,

Dippers, rollers, a single red canary, waiting
To be found a mate; they have all chosen
To sing in their cage. From three in the morning
They're at it: opera, jazz, chorale—

Better, he says, *than yer nightingale, any day.*
I'd set 'em free, she tells me quietly, *only I know*
They wouldn't live. She sees I find her hard
To understand. Precise control has left
Her lips and tongue. She pitches as she lumbers

The deck of her world, the trim new stairless house.
The canaries are nesting, their young are hatched.
She tells me she can't bear to look at them.
I watch her lifting her *stupid* left leg

Into a new position. He spends
A lot of time in the garden. The new small pond
Is his work, where the fine fat red fish swim.
Evening: the birds are chanting a sort of requiem.

Bronwen

Not an exacting shopping-list: lambs,
Birds, wildflowers, a walk, a whiff
Of Gloucestershire's April. She'd scraped together
A day for it, came provided
With entrance fee: whisky she couldn't afford,

We guessed. Not little Nell, remotely pathetic,
But tough Aussie Bron from her Brixton squat,
Wasting her wits in a clerical dead-end,
Horizon the push-bike's two-mile circuit,
Her calling the comrades, the Party, the Trots.

So we walked. She played childhood,
Mystified lambs with human bleating,
Frisked a hill-top folly, scaled drystone walls
(Sorting out the wool trade, of course, quick to note
Capitalist mansions; but cryptic violets too).

Bit short on graffiti round here?
Shot all the vandals, have they?

I introduced dog's mercury. Germander speedwell
She found for herself. How did she know it?
None grows in Brisbane, not much in Brixton.

'*Speedwell, shy blue flower of the hedgerow*
With the white eye,' she said. *I just knew it.*
Spent most of my life reading Brontës and that lot.
They're always on about your countryside, your flowers,
Sorta thing you don't forget, she said.

Unauthorised Version

(for Elma Mitchell)

'Martha was cumbered about much serving, and came to him, and said, Lord, dost thou not care that my sister hath left me to serve alone? bid her therefore that she help me. And Jesus answered and said unto her, Martha, Martha, thou art careful and troubled about many things: but one thing is needful: and Mary hath chosen that good part.'

St Luke 10, vv 38–42

Of course he meant it kindly. I know that.
I know Josh—as well as anyone can know
The Son of God. All the same, he slipped up
Over this one. After all, a Son is only a son
When you come to think about it. And this
Was between sisters. Marty and me,
We understand each other. For instance, when Lazzie died,
We didn't need to spell it out between us,
Just knew how to fix the scenario
So Josh could do his bit—raising Lazzie, I mean,
From the dead. He has his own way of doing things,
Has to muddle people first, so then the miracle
Comes as a miracle. If he'd just walked in
When Lazzie was ill, and said *OK, Lazzie,*
You're off the sick list now—that'd have lacked *impact.*
But all this weeping, and groaning, and moving of stones,
And praying in public, and Mart saying *I believe etcetera,*
Then *Lazarus, come forth!* and out comes Lazzie
In his shroud. Well, even a halfwit could see
Something out of the ordinary was going on.
But this *was* just ordinary. A lot of company,
A lot of hungry men, not many helpers,
And Mart had a go at me in front of Josh,
Saying *I'm all on my own out there. Can't you*
Tell that sister of mine to take her finger out,
And lend a hand? Well, the thing about men is,
They don't realise how *temperamental* good cooks are.
And Mart is very good. Believe you me.
She was just blowing her top. No harm in it.

I knew that. But then Josh gives her
This monumental dressing-down, and really,
It wasn't fair. The trouble with theology is, it features
Too much miraculous catering. Those ravens feeding Elijah,
For instance. I ask you! They'd have been far more likely
To *eat* him. And all those heaven-sent fast-food take-aways—
Quail, and manna, and that. And Josh himself—
The famous fish-butty picnic, and that miraculous
Draught of fishes. What poor old Mart could have done with
Was a miraculous draught of coffee and sandwiches
Instead of a ticking-off. And the men weren't much help.
Not a *thank you* among them, and never a thought
Of help with the washing-up.

Don't get me wrong. Of course I love Josh,
Wonder, admire, believe. He knows I do.
But to give Marty such a rocket
As if she was a Pharisee, or that sort of type,
The ones he has it in for. It wasn't right.
Still, Josh himself, as I said—well, he *is* only
The Son of God, not the Daughter; so how could he know?
And when it comes to the truth, I'm Marty's sister.
I was there; I heard what was said, and
I knew what was meant. The men will write it up later
From their angle, of course. But this is me, Mary,
Setting the record straight.

Gaudy Ladies

The pianist is young, appassionata. She has anarchist's hair.
She flings bright splinters of music, she glitters with promise.

They sit, dazed by *saumon, contrefilet,*
Vacherine aux fraises, delicacies their post-war non-youth

Never imagined, sit tired, the kind faces ready but blurred.
Were they once bright, savage? Was the easily manageable hair

Once eloquent? Did it get kissed in the bike sheds
At 11.15 curfew? Will her face acquire

Their lined sockets, their patient bones,
Their willingness to try to understand? O once they were

Rash, lovely, courted; I wondered at their verve,
Their Bodleian love-letters, unsolicited roses, the skeletons

They hung as knockers on their doors.

REMAINS

Nativities

Godlings are born racily.

They are excavated
Into life by the strong licks
Of the world-cow, suckled
By goats, mares, wolves.

Blossom of oak, blossom of broom,
Blossom of meadowsweet
Go to their making.

They erupt through the paternal
Skull fully armed, hatch from an egg,
Or appear, foam-born,
In Cyprus, in a shell,
Wearing a great deal of hair
And nothing else.

This one arrived
At the time of the early lambs
By means of the usual channels.

Bakerloo

The Iron Duke's last battle ended here
On this dull plain. The thin brown line
Wobbled a bit (Baker's Irregulars
Being better at one over the eight
Than forming fours). Then at their general's
Offensive challenge *Come on, scum—*
Oh, for some old Etonians! they rallied
Among the hansom cabs, firing through fog.
The Old Guard fell. Napoleon's retreat
From London started here. The wolfish men
Of Kent and Surrey picked off stragglers;
The harsh Home Counties winter took its toll;
Not many French returned from Bakerloo.

A literary place, as well. The scene
Of Conan Doyle's most chilling mystery:
The Hound of Quatre Bras.

Garden Planning

The garden seeds itself, and weaves and spins
A web, a maze, a snare.

Below becomes the way in, where hunting
Buttercups throttle with

Claw feet, and bindweed is biding its time,
Dangling slack as a noose.

More civilized mint advances neatly,
Pawn by indigo pawn.

Violent foxgloves gang up in crannies;
They have rape in their heads.

Limp goosegrass forces its mucous kisses
On more upright neighbours,

And nettle, straightforward barbarian,
Blots opposition

With a wag of green beards. Only tulips
Counter-attack, steadfast

And stiff as the Old Guard at Waterloo,
Erect, correct, scarlet,

Stalking above the delinquent chaos
With their formal statement

That somebody once created this garden,
And there was a design.

Unfinished Chronicle

(for Mick North and Janni Howker)

1. 1938

A slack year on the estate, the men
Hanging about idle. Mrs Pretty set them
To dig the heathy tumps outside the garden.

In this year the Germans marched
Into Austria, and they held it.

Basil, the one with the gift, *had a profound feeling*
(Says authority) *for the local soil.* Grew wedded to it.
If e'd ad is bed (says gardener Jack), *e'd ave slept*
Out there in the trench.

In this year also wise rulers in Europe
Met at Munich and spoke for peace.

Three mounds opened. Strange things found
In a boatgrave. *I was a green hand*
(Says Jack), *didn't rightly understand*
The value of the things.

2. 1939

In this year Adolf the leader sent men
Into Bohemia, and they held it.

They trenched the highest barrow, found
The bows of a great ship. Experts came,
Under the darkening skies of the world, to see
What hid at Sutton Hoo.

In this year also the men of Italy
Marched into Albania, and they held it.

The archaeologist spoke. *We might*
As well have a bash (said he, being young),
So a bash was what we had.

In the Bull pub at Woodbridge they stayed,
Clever, lanky young men with prewar haircuts;
Eminent, emeritus now, with their pasts behind them,
Retired, superseded, dead. And the gold
Came out of the earth bright and shining
As the day it went in.

In this year also Adolf the leader
And Benedict the leader swore to keep faith.
Men called it the pact of steel.

The winds of that year blew Redwald's flaked bones
Over the fields of his kingdom. Gold leaf also
Floated away in that weather.
Potent treasures were packed in boxes and tins
Scrounged from chemists and grocers. It was all borne
From the great ship by an elderly Ford
Which ran out of petrol outside the gates
Of the British Museum.

In this year also the men of Russia swore
That they would not fight against the Germans.
Both sides set their hands to it.

Learned clerks counted and cossetted
The awesome things, and they were stacked
In Aldwych underground for the duration.

In this year also the men of Germany
Marched into Poland, and they held it.
Then the rulers of England and France,
Who were handfast, defied the Germans,
And there was open war.

Long enough ago.

Now Mrs Pretty is dead, who loyally gave
The royal lot to the nation. Gardener Jack
And brown-fingered Basil died too, no doubt;
We have no records of them. But high to this day
In Londonchester looms the High King's regalia,
Sword, sceptre, shield, helm, drinking horns and harp,
Patched and polished, explained, made innocent, aimless.

Behind glass, air-conditioned, they wait in their own way
For what comes next:
another inhumation?
another finding?
another year?

U.A. Fanthorpe was born in Kent in 1929 and educated at Oxford. After many years teaching, several as Head of English at Cheltenham Ladies' College, she became a 'middle-aged drop-out' and began working as a clerk-receptionist in a Bristol hospital. In 1980 she won third prize in the massive Observer/Arvon/South Bank Show poetry competition judged by Charles Causley, Seamus Heaney, Ted Hughes and Philip Larkin. More recently she was awarded one of the two £1,000 Travelling Scholarships for 1983 by The Society of Authors. Between 1983 and 1985 she held an Arts Council Writer's Fellowship at S.Martin's College, Lancaster. In 1987 she won a Hawthornden Scholarship and became the Northern Arts Literary Fellow based at the Universities of Durham and Newcastle upon Tyne. Her home is in Gloucestershire.